WATCH WHAT YOU SAY

THE POWER OF THE SPOKEN WORD : REVISED

PAMELA J. THOMAS

RUACH PRESS , LLC

Unless otherwise indicated, all Scripture quotations are taken from the *King James Version of the Bible*.

Scripture quotations marked (AMP) are taken from *The Amplified Bible*. *The Amplified Bible, Old Testament* copyright © 1965, 1987 by the Zondervan Corporation. *The Amplified New Testament* © 1954, 1958,1987 by the Lochman Foundation. Used by Permission. Please note that Ruach Press LLC, publishing style capitalizes certain pronouns in Scripture that refer to the Father, Son, and Holy Spirit, and may differ from some publishers' styles.

Watch What you Say: The Power of the Spoken Word: Revised Edition

ISBN 978-1-7361511-0-5

Copyright © 2020-Pamela J. Thomas

Cover Design by Marsha Hedgeman

All rights reserved. No part of this book may be reproduced in any form without written permission from the publisher and author. Except for use in any review, the reproduction or utilization of this work in whole or part in any form by an electronic, mechanical or other means, now known or hereafter invented, including xerography, photocopying and recording, or in any formation storage or retrieval system, is forbidden without the written permission of the publisher and author.

Published by:

Ruach Press, LLC

P.O. Box 55502

Indianapolis, Indiana 46220

RuachPress@protonmail.com

I dedicate this book to my late mother, Ollie Mildred Thomas who always encouraged me to be the very best that I could be in whatever I chose to do. She exemplified what it meant to be a follower of Jesus in every area of her life. She was my greatest mentor. I will always love you mother.

ACKNOWLEDGMENTS

I want to thank the Lord for moving in my heart to revise this book with added information and insights to bless the Body of Christ.

Many thanks to Marsha Hedgeman who helped me in numerous ways in the publication of this book. Her help is greatly appreciated.

I wish to thank all of you who have chosen to read what is written within these pages. May the blessing of the Lord be upon you as you not only read, but act accordingly.

CONTENTS

Preface   vii
Introduction   ix

1. God is a Speaking God   1
2. Speak in Agreement with the Word   5
3. Linking the Mouth and the Heart   15
4. Speak Life and not Death   25
5. Truth or Fact?   39
6. Angels Listen to Your Words   53
7. Speak the Word Daily   63

Appendix A   75
Bibliography   83
About the Author   85
Contact Information   87

PREFACE

At the time of completing this book, our world is in chaos. The nations have been shut down because of the Covid-19 virus. The United States of America has been hit particularly hard. In addition to deaths caused by the virus, there are fires on the West coast, flood's triggered by hurricanes on the East Coast, riots over racial injustice, loss of jobs, and the list goes on.

Fear has engulfed our society and, many are in depressions and "giving-up attitudes". This is exactly the right time for the people of God, to arise and be who He has called us to be, overcomers and bearers of the Good News. How we speak and act during this time is key in extending hope and peace to the world around us. It is vital to watch what you say. Let the message of this book become personal so God can use you to speak life and hope in these desperate times.

INTRODUCTION

This book has been written for the body of Christ. The intent is to create an awareness of the important role that words have in one's personal destiny and the fulfillment of the will of God in this earth realm. In the Sermon on the Mount, Jesus taught His disciples to pray that God's will be done on earth as it is in heaven. For this to be fulfilled, we as people of God must speak those things that will bring about His manifested will in the earth.

Many of the people of God do not realize the import of their words on their personal life, and the world in which they live. As you read this book, you will learn the importance of speaking right words. You will also learn how to train yourself to speak right words in the face of contrary situations. As sons of God we have been promised abundant life. There is no reason we should live beneath our privilege as heirs of God and joint heirs with Jesus Christ. We are to take on the nature of our Father God, who framed the world with His words.

It is also the intent of this book to clarify areas of misunderstanding about confession of the Word of God. There has been a great deal of misunderstanding in this area, both in the past and at present. Faith in God's Word and confession of the word go together like hand in glove and represent a vital link in the fulfillment of the promises of God in our lives. You cannot speak of one without referring to the other. Our faith is built up and sustained through right speaking and acting on the Word. The Holy Bible is the standard for clarification and our guidebook for growth and maturity in all aspects of our Christian walk. It is the Word of God which will be referenced throughout these pages as we focus on right speaking.

It is my prayer, dear reader, that you will be blessed by reading, *Watch What You Say: The Power of the Spoken Word*, and will become adept at speaking right words which edify, empower and bring blessing to yourself and others.

1

GOD IS A SPEAKING GOD

As we begin our journey of watching what we say, it is necessary to go back in time and look at how God operated when He created the heavens and the earth. In the Genesis account, God created everything by the spoken word. The sun, moon, stars, the sea, dry land, animal life and vegetable life, were created as He spoke them into existence with the words, "*Let there be... and it was so.*" Hebrews 11:3 says, "*By faith we understand the worlds [during the successive ages] were framed (fashioned, put in order, and equipped for their intended purpose) by the word of God, so that what we see was not made out of things which are visible* (AMP). Nothing existed before God spoke it into existence. The entire universe exists because of the word God spoke in the beginning. Contrary to what some believe, the world did not come into existence out of nowhere but exists according to God's spoken word. The earth spins on its axis, which motion began when God commanded it to do so.

Man was the last of God's creation as recorded in Genesis 1 verses 26 and 27: *And God said, Let us make man in our image, after our likeness: and let them have dominion over the fish of the sea, and over the fowl of the air, and over the cattle, and over all the earth, and over every creeping thing that creepeth upon the earth. So God created man in his own image, in the image of God created he him; male and female created he them.* The word *image* in this scripture is the Hebrew word *tselem (tseh´lem)* and means, representative figure, or resemblance.[1] The word *likeness* is the Hebrew word *dmuth (dem-ooth´)* and means resemblance, manner, similitude.[2] From these definitions, we understand that God made man to resemble Himself. He (God) is a speaking spirit and He created man to be a speaking being. As such, the words man speaks can shape his environment and ultimately affect his destiny.

What God created in the beginning through his spoken word was, according to scripture, good and very good (Gen. 1:12, 18, 21, 25, 31). If we are to be representatives of our God, we must speak His Word to change contrary situations that work against us, so that what the devil means for evil, God will work for our good. The scripture states in Romans 8:28, "*And we know that all things work together for good to them that love God, to them who are the called according to his purpose.*"

Not understanding the importance of right speaking has caused much damage both individually and corporately to the Body of Christ. The scripture in Hosea 4:6 says, *My people are destroyed for the lack of knowledge.* We avoid destruction when we learn how to speak God's Word. St. John 15:7 says, "*If ye abide in me, and my words abide in you, ye shall ask what ye will, and it shall be done unto you."* Note especially that receiving from God is contingent upon allowing His words to abide or be a constant part of your speech.

Words are powerful and can work for or against you. More often than not, the people of God are speaking words that work against them instead of those that work on their behalf. Some have blamed God for situations that have occurred in their lives, not realizing that the negative words they have constantly spoken and acted upon have brought about these circumstances.

God confounded the language of the people in Genesis 11 who were building the Tower of Babel. These people set a goal of building a tower that would reach into heaven. The construction of this tower would give them notoriety by its accomplishment as recorded in Genesis 11:4, *And they said, Go to, let us build us a city and a tower, whose top may reach unto heaven; and let us make us a name, lest we be scattered abroad upon the face of the whole earth.* God gave them different languages so they could not understand one another and by their words and unity of purpose accomplish what was contrary to His will. The scripture says in Genesis 11:6, *"And the Lord said, Behold, the people is one, and they have all one language; and this they begin to do: and now nothing will be restrained from them, which they have imagined to do."* They lost the power of words to create their reality and were scattered abroad. They abandoned building the tower. According to the preceding scripture, they would have accomplished their purpose had they been allowed to speak and encourage one another in their native language.

The words we speak can be life-giving or destroying, the impact of which is noted in a scripture that you will read throughout this book which says, "Death *and life are in the power of the tongue: and they that love it shall eat the fruit thereof (Proverbs 18:21)*." As people made in God's image and likeness, we must learn to speak God's Word by applying it to every aspect of our lives. Speaking His word is of the utmost importance as we strive to live the abundant life that He promises to those who make Him Lord of their lives. So, follow along with me as we explore together in chapter 2 the importance of speaking in agreement with God's Word.

Endnotes

1. James Strong, *The New Strong's Exhaustive Concordance of the Bible*, Hebrew #6754.
2. Ibid., Hebrew #1823.

2

SPEAK IN AGREEMENT WITH THE WORD

The biblical word for speaking in agreement with what God has said is the word *confession*. For many years as a Christian, I always heard the word confession in relation to one's guilt or sins. It never occurred to me that the word could have another meaning. As I studied and sought God for greater knowledge of His Word, I discovered that the word *confession* meant more than the admission of guilt.

In the language of the New Testament, the word translated confession is the Greek word *homologeo* and has a twofold meaning. One meaning is to confess by way of admitting oneself guilty of what one is accused, and the other meaning is to speak the same thing; agree with; declare openly by way of speaking out freely.[1] The word *confession* encompasses the idea of acknowledging guilt, as well as speaking those things that are in agreement with the Word of God. There is a place for confession in terms of admission of guilt and sin as expressed in 1 John 1:9

which tells us, "*If we confess our sins, He is faithful and just to forgive us our sins, and to cleanse us from all unrighteousness.*" Since the focus of this book pertains to speaking in agreement with the Word, it is this meaning of confession that I shall use throughout this book.

In Romans 10:10 the scripture says, "*For with the heart man believeth unto righteousness; and with the mouth confession is made unto salvation.*" Let us take a look at the word *salvation* to gain a better understanding of the word *confession*. The word *salvation* in the Greek is an all-inclusive word. It is the word "*sozo*" and means deliverance, preservation, healing, soundness and all the redemptive acts and processes.[2] Oftentimes salvation is only considered in the context of making a commitment to Jesus Christ and being filled with the Holy Spirit. However, salvation is a continuing process in which you are being saved as you continue to walk with the Lord. Therefore, when the scripture says, "*confession is made unto salvation*", it means that you can say about yourself what the Word of God declares in the areas of deliverance, preservation, healing, soundness, and any of the promises that He has spoken in His Word. Instead of talking about how weak you are and how you do not feel that you have strength to continue on, speak the words of Joel 3:10, "*... let the weak say, I am strong*", or Philippians 4:13, "*I can do all things through Christ who strengtheneth me.*" In the same sense refuse to make your lack of money, job, car, or other needs the topic of constant conversation. Agree with the Word which says, "*My God supplies all of my needs according to his riches in glory by Christ Jesus*" (Phil. 4:19). Likewise Psalms 107:2 tells us to, "*Let the redeemed of the Lord say so, whom*

He hath redeemed from the hand of the enemy." The things we are to "say so" pertain to being healed, delivered, and set free from strongholds and bondages in our lives.

Pause for a moment and consider the kind of confessions you make every day. Do you speak in agreement with the Word, or in direct opposition to it? Words are containers and they can work for your good, or they can work against you. St Matthew 12:37 says, *"For by thy words thou shalt be justified and by thy words thou shalt be condemned."* The word justified means, to declare free of blame, and condemned means to pronounce to be wrong. If we substitute these definitions into the scripture just quoted, it reads, *"For by thy words thou shalt be **declared free of blame**, and by thy words thou shalt **be pronounced wrong.**"* If we agree with the Word of God concerning His promises, we will be free of blame and can come to Him in the right way and receive. On the other hand, if we speak contrary to the Word of God where His promises are concerned, we hinder ourselves from receiving His blessings.

The children of Israel in the wilderness are good examples of wrong confession and being condemned by their words. Hebrews 4:2 says, *"...but the Word preached did not profit them, not being mixed with faith in them that heard it."* We know that they did not mix the Word with faith because of how they spoke concerning the Word God had given them. God said to them through His servant Moses,

> *For the Lord thy God bringeth thee into a good land, a land of brooks of water, of fountains and depths that spring out of valleys and*

> hills; A land of wheat, and barley, and vines, and fig trees, and pomegranates; a land of oil olive, and honey; A land wherein thou shalt eat bread without scareness, thou shalt not lack any thing in it; a land whose stones are iron, and out of whose hills thou mayest dig brass (Deuteronomy 8:7-9).

God told them that He was bringing them into a land where they would lack nothing. This land would be abundant in food, water, and whatever else they needed for their well-being. The blessing was that they would inherit the toil and labor of those who they would dispossess and would not have to start from scratch.

After sending twelve spies out to search the land God promised them, ten of them came back with a negative report. They affirmed that the land was what God said that it was, but they added the following negative statements:

> And they told him, and said, We came unto the land whither thou sentest us, and surely it floweth with milk and honey; and this is the fruit of it.
> Nevertheless the people be strong that dwell in the land, and the cities are walled, and very great: and moreover we saw the children of Anak there.
> The Amalekites dwell in the land of the south: and the Amorites dwell in the mountains:

and the Canaanites dwell by the sea, and by the coast of Jordan (Numbers 13:27-29).

They further exaggerated the report by stating that the people of the land were tall, and they appeared as grasshoppers in their own sight: *And they brought up an evil report of the land which they had searched unto the children of Israel, saying, The land, through which we have gone to search it, is a land that eateth up the inhabitants thereof; and all the people that we saw in it are men of a great stature. And there we saw the giants, the sons of Anak, which come of the giants: and we were in our own sight as grasshoppers, and so we were in their sight (Numbers 13:32-33).*

The children of Israel saw themselves differently from the way God saw them. He saw them as a conquering people whom He loved. Their ability to conquer the people of the land was not predicated on their size but rather on who God said they were and His ability to bring to pass His Word in their lives. Unlike these Israelites, we as children of God must see ourselves as God sees us and speak accordingly.

The negative words spoken by the ten spies put fear in the hearts of the people to the extent that they wept, complained, and desired to go back to Egypt. Their words of condemnation were contrary to what God said they could have. Because of their negative confession, which expressed their unbelief, God became angry with them. When God spoke to them through Moses, He let them know that as they had spoken in His ears, so would He do to them, *"How long shall I bear with this evil congregation, which murmur against me? I have heard the murmurings of* the children of Israel, which they murmur against me. Say unto them, As truly as I live, saith the Lord, as ye have spoken in mine ears, so will I do to you... (Numbers 14:27-28)." Their own words condemned them and kept them from entering the land of Promise.

Although the majority were condemned by their words, there were two of the spies, Caleb and Joshua, who were justified by their words as revealed in Numbers 14:6-9:

> *And Joshua the son of Nun, and Caleb the son of Jephunneh, which were of them that searched the land, rent their clothes:*
> *And they spake unto all the company of the children of Israel, saying, the land, which we passed through to search it, is an exceeding good land.*
> *If the Lord delight in us, then He will bring us into this land, and give it us; a land which floweth with milk and honey.*
> *Only rebel not ye against the Lord, neither fear ye the people of the land; for they are bread for us; their defense is departed from them, and the Lord is with us: fear them not.*

These men spoke words in agreement with what God promised them. As a result, God let them know that they would enter the Promised Land, and said, *"Doubtless ye shall not come into the land, concerning which I sware to make you dwell therein, save Caleb the son of Jephunneh, and Joshua the son of Nun (Numbers 14:30)."* As you follow the history of Israel, what God said would happen came to pass: Joshua and Caleb entered the Promised Land and those 20 years old and upward died in the wilderness. In fact, Joshua was God's chosen leader after the death of Moses, and the one who led the children of Israel into the land of Promise.

You can often locate people by their confession. If they believe God, it will be expressed in their words. I have had people to tell me they believed God to be their healer, provider, protector, etc. Yet in the very next breath they would speak about their condition being worse, not having money to meet their needs, being too afraid to leave the house at night or some other statement that negated what they previously said. In such cases, their belief was only mental assent to the Word. When we believe God, our speech will be in line with His Word. This is verified by the Apostle Paul in 2 Corinthians 4:13, *"We having the same spirit of faith, according as it is written, I believed, and therefore have I spoken; we also believe and therefore speak."* When we speak in agreement with the Word of God, our confessions will cause us to be justified rather than condemned by our words.

Constant confession of sickness, disease, poverty, and death gives Satan authority to bring these things to pass in your life. Do not agree with him. Ephesians 4:27 says, *"Neither give place to the devil."* When you agree with Satan, you are giving him place. I live in the Midwestern part of the United States, and during the late fall and early winter months we have what we know as the flu season. During this time lots of people become ill with cold-like symptoms of sneezing and coughing. I have heard people comment over and over when they get a few sniffles and a runny nose, "I must be getting the flu." Consequently, they end up with the flu. At the onset of symptoms, I declare the Word of God over myself. I do not give a name to the symptoms by saying that I must be getting the flu. I command symptoms to leave in the Name of Jesus, declaring that Christ has redeemed me from sickness, and I am healed by His stripes. Sometimes before I realize it, the symptoms of coughing and sneezing are manifesting in my body. It appears that cold or flu has taken hold. It may have sneaked up on me, but I refuse its right to stay in my body by speaking in agreement with the Word of God, and it leaves. When we agree with the Word, we release God's authority to fulfill His Word on our behalf.

One thing, for sure, you cannot agree with the Word if you do not know what it says. Many of the people of God suffer from what I will call a "Word deficit". They do not study the Word and meditate on it so they can counter the negative circumstances and situations that arise with confession of God's Word. Spending just a few minutes a day in the Word, and allowing it to saturate your heart and mind, will give you what you need to make positive confessions over yourself and others. As a youngster I recall memorizing passages of scripture in Sunday school and in weekday religious education, which was a part of the public-school curriculum. The scriptures I learned then are yet in my memory. Of course, times have changed in the public schools. Since the removal of the Word of God in schools, there has been a steady increase in shootings and mass killings along with an increase in sexual promiscuity, drugs and a host of other evils that are destroying our young people. The confession of the Word through reading and reciting scriptures would be a blessing to our present-day public schools.

Constant repetition of the Word causes it to get into your heart. Once the Word gets into your heart, you will begin to speak it out of your mouth. It is this crucial linking of the heart and mouth that I will examine more closely in the following chapter.

Endnotes

1. W.E. Vine, Vines Expository Dictionary of Old and New Testament Words, (Old Tappan New Jersey: Fleming H. Revell, 1981), s. v. "confession."
2. Rev. C. I. Scofield, *The Scofield Study Bible,* (New York, New York: Oxford University Press, 1909), s.v. "salvation."

3

LINKING THE MOUTH AND THE HEART

In learning how to speak in agreement with the Word of God, it is imperative to understand that the heart and the mouth are inextricably tied together. Whatever is in your heart in abundance, will be spoken out of your mouth, as confirmed in Matthew 12:34, *"... for out of the abundance of the heart, the mouth speaketh."* The interesting fact is that the words you speak program your heart to release whatever you have spoken into it. Let us take a look to see how this works.

When we speak about the heart, we are not referring to the physical organ that pumps blood through the body. Rather, we are referring to the spiritual heart, which is the innermost being, or that part of us which contains our affections, emotions, desires, passions, sensibilities, will and purpose. Proverbs 4:23 says, *"Keep thy heart with all diligence; for out of it are the issues of life."* The word *keep* is the Hebrew word *natsar* (naw-tsar) which means to guard (in a good sense), to protect, maintain.[1] We must guard or protect our heart by being diligent in refusing access to anything that could cause harm since the issues of life proceed out of it.

The word "issue" is the Hebrew word *totsaah* (to-tsaw-aw) and means an outgoing or an issuing forth.[2] In other words, out of the heart come those things that issue forth from what you have placed there. These issues vary according to what you allow in your heart. If you allow anger, jealousy, unforgiveness, bitterness or any other negative influence into your heart, you will speak accordingly. I am sure that you have heard individuals speak disparaging words against others. These words affect the person being talked about as well as the one speaking them. They affect the person talked about by the spread of damaging information to others. The person speaking these words is affected because such attitudes of heart hinder their walk with the Lord.

You cannot obey God's commandment to love others and speak hurtful words against them. The scripture tells us in Proverbs 26:22, *"The words of a talebearer are as wounds, they go down into the innermost parts of the belly."* The negative words you speak against others are like wounds, and often it takes wounds a while to heal. Sometimes they never heal. The Psalmist talks in Psalms 64:2-3 about wicked people whose words are like arrows: *"Who whet their tongue like a sword, and bend their bows to shoot their arrows, even bitter words."* The word "bitter" has the meaning of cruel, harsh or angry words. You must not be as the wicked and speak bitter words against others.

To successfully program your heart, you must speak right words. Proverbs 3:3 says, *"Let not mercy and truth forsake thee: bind them about thy neck; write them upon the table of thine heart.*" The question is, how do I write on the table of my heart? The answer comes from Psalms 45:1, "... ***my tongue** is the pen of a ready writer.*" It is the words you speak which write on your heart. Just as words written on paper convey thoughts, likewise, words you speak convey the thoughts of your heart. More succinctly, the heart expresses what the mouth has programmed into it, whether for good or evil.

The scripture tells us in Matthew 12:35, "*A good man out of the good treasure of the heart bringeth forth good things: and an evil man out of the evil treasure bringeth forth evil things.*" The word "treasure" in the Greek is the word *thesaurus (thay-sow-ros)* and means deposit.[3] The word "deposit" has the meaning of storing things somewhere. If we inserted this word in the scripture it would read, "*a good man out of the **good deposit** of the heart bringeth forth good things: and an evil man out of **the evil deposit** bringeth forth evil things.*" Jesus spoke a parable which explains how deposits are made in the heart. It is the parable of the sower. In this parable a sower planted seed into four kinds of soil which represented the heart. In interpreting this parable to His disciples, Jesus said, "*The sower soweth the word (Mark 4:14).*" It is the Word of God that we sow in our hearts by speaking it forth from our mouths. It brings forth a harvest of good things in our lives. Conversely, when we speak words contrary to God's Word, it brings forth the negative in our lives. This follows the principle already mentioned that the tongue writes on our hearts, for good or for bad.

I can remember an old saying I heard as a child that,

"A drunken person speaks his or her sober thoughts." What this means is that when alcohol has taken its toll on an individual and there are no longer any inhibitions, whatever the person really feels or thinks about someone or something, they will say without reservation. This statement has been accurate as I have observed it acted out true to the Word of God, that whatever we sow in our hearts will be spoken out of our mouths.

Mercy and truth are what we are to write on our hearts according to Proverbs 3:3 which says, *Let not mercy and truth forsake thee: bind them about thy neck; write them upon the table of thine heart.* If we write these on our hearts, we will not speak negatively about others. Instead of tearing people down, we will build them up. We must remind ourselves that God has mercy on us and does not dismiss us when we do not measure up but gives us the chance to go in a right direction. The scripture in James 2:13 tells us that *"mercy rejoices against judgment"* because to be merciful is far better than pronouncing judgment on others. Instead of dismissing others or severing friendships when things do not go our way, we show mercy through speaking words of understanding and forgiveness coupled with acts of kindness and love.

It is the truth of God's Word that we will write on our hearts, and when we are dealing with others, we will speak His truth in love. Parents, instead of always expressing how your children appear to you, speak what you desire for them. Isaiah 54:13 says, "And all thy children shall be taught of the Lord; and great shall be the peace of thy children." You teach as you speak the Word over them, show them by example, and expose them to the preaching and teaching of the Word. This goes right along with Proverbs 22:6, *"Train up a child in the way he should go: and when he is old, he will not depart from it."*

If your children forget their chores and hang out with their friends, chastise them but do not continually say to them that they will never be responsible. Begin to speak that they may not be showing it now, but they will learn responsibility. When children associate with the wrong crowd and end up in inappropriate behaviors, you need to speak the word of God over them proclaiming their deliverance instead of telling them they will never amount to anything. The truth of God's Word will write on their hearts and change their behavior. Now, they may not change in a day, but do not give up on them. God's Word will not return void according to Isaiah 55:11, *"... it will accomplish that which He pleases and will prosper in the thing for which it was sent."* Parents, you have the responsibility of speaking wholesome and encouraging words over your children.

You can always tell how you have programmed your heart when a sudden surprising situation occurs. For example, when you stump your toe or hit your knee, your response to the pain is what you have programmed into your heart. Do you respond with an expletive, or by calling on Jesus? What do you say when someone cuts you off in traffic? Do you bless the person or curse them out? The scripture says in James 3:11-12, *"Doth a fountain send forth at the same place sweet water and bitter? Can the fig tree, my brethren, bear olive berries? either a vine, figs? so can no fountain both yield salt water and fresh."* Whatever you "write" into your heart will be what issues forth. It is too late to say after the fact that "I didn't mean to say that", or, "The bad words just slipped out." You spoke what was in your heart and your regrets will not erase the wrong words you released. You can repent for the words spoken and determine not to repeat such speech in the future.

Crisis situations will also reveal what is in your heart. Some years ago, I read an account of a plane crash in which two planes collided on takeoff. This account is recorded in the book, *Terror at Tenerife,* written by a man who was a believer and a passenger on one of the planes involved in the crash.[4] Prior to the flight, his mother prayed that the Lord would grant him traveling mercies. He tells that when the plane caught on fire and the people were being burned by the fire; they spoke what was in their heart in abundance. Many of them spoke horrible curse words with some even cursing God. He said that when he saw the fire hurling towards him, he spoke the Word, "By the shed blood of Jesus, I stand on the Word of God." He continued to speak the phrase, "I stand on your Word", and miraculously ended up outside on the wing of the plane through a hole created by the collision. From that point he jumped off the wing to the ground with minor injuries. In the book he makes the comment, "As I look back at it I know that through my having trusted on the Word of Jesus, He had confirmed that I was an heir, a joint heir, of His love. I had learned that His Word is good in any crisis." New meaning to His promise, "all things are possible to them that believe."[5] The Word of God was written on his heart so that in the time of crisis what he spoke brought life.

The point is, you cannot wait until a crisis comes to

determine how you will respond. If you begin now to program your heart with right words, what issues forth will come from the good deposits of your heart and will cause you to reap a harvest of the wonderful promises of God. It is what you speak and believe which will determine your destiny. Will you have a life of abundance as the scripture states in John 10:10, or one filled with negativity and lack? Carefully consider these questions in the light of how you speak. As the Psalmist David said, *"Let the words of my mouth, and the meditations of my heart be acceptable in thy sight, O Lord, my strength, and my redeemer (Psalm 19:14)."* Include this scripture in your daily prayer to God. You might even add another scripture to this one found in Psalms 141:3 which says, *"Set a watch, O Lord, before my mouth; keep the door of my lips."* The words that issue forth from your mouth can only be acceptable to God as they mirror His Word. On the following pages you will find *Prayers for Right Speaking*. These prayers focus on the aforementioned scriptures. You can pray them over yourself daily, and remember, what you allow into your heart will be spoken out of your mouth.

Prayers for Right Speaking

Psalm 19:14
Let the words of my mouth, and the meditation of my heart, be acceptable in thy sight, O Lord, my strength, and my redeemer.

Heavenly Father, in the Name of Jesus I come before you asking for your help to speak in a manner that honors you. I do not want to program into my heart such things as gossip, slander, anger, malice, jealousy, or anything else of a negative and hurtful nature. I repent of wrong speaking. Cleanse me by the washing of the water of your Word, and help me speak life-producing, uplifting and edifying words about others as well as myself.

Help me apply your Word to all aspects of my life and speak it over myself and others continually. I ask this with faith that you will bring it to pass in my life because your word says that, "if we ask anything according to your will you hear us, and if you hear us, we know that we have the petitions that we desire of you" (1John 5: 14-15). Thank you for granting my request. Amen.

∼

Psalm 141:3
Set a watch, O Lord, before my mouth; keep the door of my lips.

Father, in the Name of Jesus, set a Holy Spirit watch over my tongue so I will not sin with my mouth. Help me to always be aware of what I say as I seek to please You in all areas of my life. You said, Lord, that a word spoken in due season is good (Prov. 15:23). Help me speak words of blessing and always speak the truth in love. I realize that I cannot do this on my own, but with your help, I can do all things.

I repent for all the times I have been careless with my words and ask that you forgive me. This includes the times I have spoken, knowing that the words that came forth were hurtful and not befitting a child of God. In the Name of Jesus, I break the power of negative and unscriptural words, prayers or pronouncements that have been spoken against me and that I have spoken against others. I render all such speech null and void by the precious Blood of Jesus.

I commit my speech to you Lord this day, believing and thanking you for granting my request in Jesus' Name. Amen.

Endnotes

1. James Strong, *The New Strong's Exhaustive Concordance of the Bible,* Hebrew #5341.
2. Ibid., Hebrew #8444.
3. Ibid., Greek #2344.
4. George Otis, with Norman Williams, *Terror at Tenerife,* (Van Nuys, California: Bible Voice, 1977).
5. Ibid, 68.

4

SPEAK LIFE AND NOT DEATH

Jesus made a powerful statement in John 6:63 when He said, *"It is the spirit that quickeneth; the flesh profiteth nothing: the words that I speak unto you, they are spirit, and they are life."* He is telling us in this scripture that it is the Spirit of God that gives life, which is resident in His Word. He demonstrated the life-giving quality of the Word through the miracles, signs, and wonders that He performed. He healed the blind, lame, demon possessed, and all manner of sickness and disease. In some instances, He simply said, "Be healed", or "Come out." In others, He spoke the Word or gave instructions allowing the people an opportunity to act on their faith. For example, in the case of the ten lepers, Jesus told them to go show themselves to the priest, and scripture records that "as they went, they were cleansed" (Luke 17:14).

In the account of the Roman centurion we have yet

another example of the life-giving Word (Matthew 8:5-13). In this passage, the centurion came to Jesus on behalf of his servant who was sick. Jesus was going to travel to where the servant was to heal him, but the centurion, who understood authority, asked Jesus to *"speak the word only"* and his servant would be healed. Jesus marveled at his faith, declaring that He had not seen this kind of faith in Israel. He told the centurion to go and, as he believed, so it would be. The result was that his servant was healed. Jesus spoke life into the servant and although the centurion was a Gentile, his faith in the words of Jesus superseded that of the religious Jews of his time. He placed his confidence in the authority that rested in the life-giving words of Jesus.

The book of Proverbs has a lot to say about words and the effect that they have for life or death. In Chapter 18 verse 21 the scripture says, *"Death and life are in the power of the tongue: and they that love it shall eat the fruit thereof."* This scripture applies to what we say about ourselves and what we say about others. As mentioned earlier, parents can bless or curse their children by the words they speak. If they are constantly telling their children they are stupid, can do nothing right, or will never amount to anything, they may very well end up believing these negative statements about themselves, or have a complex because of such speaking. Then again, there are many successful people today because the adults and other significant people in their lives spoke life-giving words over them.

How many believers in Jesus Christ today will speak the Word of God and believe that what they say will come to pass? Mark 11:23 says, *"For verily I say unto you, That whosoever **shall say unto this mountain**, Be thou removed, and be thou cast into the sea; and shall not doubt in his heart, but shall believe that those **things which he saith** shall come to pass; he shall have **whatsoever he saith*** (emphasis mine)." Notice in this passage that the words "say" and "saith", are mentioned three times. Jesus emphasized the point that your words are of paramount importance to receive by faith. He used this passage in one of His "teachable moments" with his disciples. Prior to speaking these words, he cursed a fig tree by saying to it, "... *No man eat fruit of thee hereafter forever* (Mark 11:14)." This occurred as he and His disciples were on their way to Jerusalem. The word "cursed" means to speak evil about or pray against. Upon returning from Jerusalem, Peter noticed that the fig tree which Jesus cursed had dried up by the root (Mark 11:21). This was a demonstration of the truth that death and life are in the power of the words you speak. As an expression of Jesus in the earth, we can speak words of life that bring healing, deliverance, and wholeness because His Word is spirit and life. We can also speak words against the negative influences that oppose God's will for our lives by binding the work of the enemy and choosing to walk according to His Word.

There is an adage that many of us have heard which says, "Sticks and stones may break my bones, but words will never hurt me." This statement is totally false because words can destroy. Proverbs 18:25 says, *"A man who bears false witness against his neighbor is like a heavy sledgehammer and a sword and a sharp arrow (AMP)."* False witness in this scripture refers to untrue words spoken against someone, which are like a sledgehammer, a sword, and a sharp arrow. These tools of destruction can inflict great harm to the point of destroying someone. In like manner, negative words spoken about someone can destroy their character and totally change the way others view them. The bottom-line being words can hurt you.

Dr. Caroline Leaf expresses in scientific language how negative words can affect attitudes when she says, "The words you speak feed back into the magic trees of the mind, reinforcing the memory they came from. When you make negative statements, you release negative chemicals. These lead to negative memories that grow stronger and become negative strongholds that control your attitude and life."[1] This understanding further highlights the deleterious effect that negative words can have in your life.

The unfortunate consequence of the destructive power of words is that once they are released, you cannot recall them. It is like releasing feathers into the air that you can never recover because the wind has carried them away to places unknown. You can apologize for saying the wrong thing, but the damage is already done. It is only through repentance that we are forgiven and cleansed by the blood of Jesus (1John 1:9).

Jesus demonstrated the power inherent in the spoken word time and again. In the eighteenth chapter of John, when the soldiers came to arrest Him, He responded to their question of His identity with the words, "I AM He." The force of these words caused the men to fall backward to the ground (John 18:5-6). The essence of Jesus is wrapped up in the words "I AM". He is everything that you need Him to be. If you recall in the Old Testament when Moses was to go before Pharaoh, he asked God who should he say had sent him. God's reply was, *"I AM THAT I AM: and he said Thus shalt thou say unto the children of Israel, I AM hath sent me unto you* (Exodus 3:13-14)." The very words "I AM" contain power in the sense that God can and will be whatever He needs to be in our life situations. The weight of who He is causes the whole of creation to bow to Him. He is truly the Almighty God!

As followers of Jesus, the words we speak can be as weapons used against the assaults of the enemy. Jesus did so in the time he spent on earth. One such occasion is recorded in Matthew chapter 4 and is often known as the temptation of Jesus. Every time Satan tempted Him, Jesus countered with the weapon of the Word. The following scriptures further demonstrate that words spoken are weapons that can destroy the enemy:

> *And He had in his right hand seven stars: and out of his mouth went a sharp twoedged sword, and his countenance was as the sun shineth in his strength (Revelation 1:16).*

> *And out of his mouth goeth a sharp word, that with it he should smite the nations: and he shall rule them with a rod of iron: and he treadeth the winepress of the fierceness and wrath of Almighty God (Revelation 19:15).*

> *And he hath made my mouth like a sharp sword; in the shadow of his hand hath he*

> hid me, and made me a polished shaft; in
> his quiver hath he hid me (Isaiah 49:2).

When I understood the importance of speaking life instead of death, I watched closely what I said. I noticed that there were various occasions where I would use the word "death." Prior to this time, I just considered this way of speaking as normal expression. I am sure that there are many of you reading this book who use or have used some of these same expressions such as:

- "That scared me to death."
- "Tickled me to death."
- "I just love you to death."
- "I am just dying to see...."
- "My back, arm, etc. etc., is killing me."

Some may say that it is ridiculous to think there is anything wrong with using the word "death" in this manner. However, as people of God we are to speak wholesome words that minister life. None of the above phrases speak life. We can characterize them as idle words. Matthew 12:36 says, *"But I say unto you, That every idle word that men shall speak, they shall give account thereof in the day of judgment."* The word "idle" is the Greek word, *argos (ar-gos)* and means ineffective or worthless.[2] We must not waste our time speaking words of no positive value to ourselves or others.

Speaking sarcastically is an example of the use of idle words. If a person is known to be stingy, you should not refer to them in conversation as, "the most generous person", to make a point of their stinginess. By doing so, you are making fun of them and, speaking an untruth. In the same sense, you must be careful of using flattery to be recognized by someone or to manipulate them for your purposes. The Bible says in Proverbs 26:28, *"A lying tongue hateth those that are afflicted by it; and a flattering mouth worketh ruin.* When you use flattery, you are really being unjust and unrighteous because you are deceiving the person to whom you are speaking. You are saying things that you do not mean, to gain an advantage or favor from the individual. A better understanding of flattery is clarified in the Amplified translation of Jude 1:16 in referring to those who speak ungodly, and says, "...*their talk is boastful and arrogant, [and they claim to] admire men's persons and pay people flattering compliments to gain advantage."* Let us not join the company of those who fill their speech with idle words. The world is negative enough without adding to the mix meaningless and deceitful speech that does not edify or encourage ourselves or others.

Ephesians 4:29 expresses ineffective speech in another way and says, *"Let no corrupt communication proceed out of your mouth but that which is good to the use of edifying that it may minister grace unto the hearers."* The word "corrupt" is the Greek word *sapros (sap-ros)* and means bad or worthless.[3] When you are speaking of death or dying as previously mentioned, you are using corrupt words especially if you mean the opposite. This scripture tells us we should speak words of encouragement that build up and bring favor or grace to the listener. If you desire prosperity in finances, you cannot constantly talk about being broke and unable to afford the things you need. You must instead speak those things you desire for them to manifest in your life.

There is a church in my city which has on its front lawn an announcement sign which reads, "The church which will love you to life." The important principle involved in this statement is that the very nature of love is life-giving. It would be wonderful if more of us would love people to life rather than to death. Our churches could not hold the people that would come if love were apparent in every aspect of our operation. Constantly speaking death and referring to it will not produce life. We must speak life to reap the same.

Wrong speaking can ensnare you according to Proverbs 6:2 which says, "*Thou art snared with the words of thy mouth, thou art taken with the words of thy mouth.*" The Amplified version of this verse reads, "*You are snared with the words of your lips, you are caught in the speech of your mouth.*" The word *snared* means to *catch in a trap*. The illustration can be used of a trap that is laid for an animal. The animal steps on an area unaware of the presence of a trap until it is too late. It is caught and ensnared in the trap. In the same sense, many do not realize the impact of negative, fear-filled, faith destroying words that entrap them as they are constantly uttered. Such speech as, "My memory is terrible, I just can't seem to remember anything", or "I must be getting Alzheimer's", are negative statements which will ensnare you. Instead of your memory getting better, you will continue to forget. When I am speaking to someone and have a problem with recall, I say, "It will come to me", and continue speaking. Without fail, what I was trying to recall comes to mind either as I am speaking or shortly thereafter.

The book of James chapter three speaks of the tongue in several ways. He begins by saying that *"it is a fire, a world of iniquity"* (James 3:6). All of us are aware of the damage that fire can produce once it is ignited. It has the potential of destroying any object, material, or person in its path. If unattended and allowed to run its course, it will wreak havoc. This is exactly the way the tongue is. If there is no attention or discretion given to what is being said, the result can be confusion, conflict, strife, and a host of other negative consequences.

James also compares the tongue to the rudder of a ship, and to a bit that is placed in a horse's mouth (James 3:3-4). The rudder although a tiny part of a ship steers it in the direction it should go just as the bit in the horse's mouth turns it in the desired direction of the rider. Imagine with me for a moment both steering mechanisms in relation to the tongue. When you speak right words, you are going in a positive direction but if you speak negative words, your direction changes and you will never reach the desired destination of blessing and fulfillment of destiny. You see, the tongue controls your direction in life. If you are constantly speaking negative, harmful, fear-laden, destiny destroying, hurtful words, you are setting the course for a life which will spiral down in misfortune and defeat. The admonition in 1Peter 3:10-11 says, *"For he that will love life, and see good days, let him **refrain his tongue from evil**, and his lips that they speak no guile* (emphasis mine)." Peter is saying in this verse, "Stop speaking wrong words!"

James continues in verse 8 of chapter 3 and tells us that the tongue is, *"... an unruly evil, full of deadly poison."* Most of us know that poison can spread infection throughout the body and result in death. In the same way, wrong speech is like poison affecting all areas of our lives. Therefore, we must allow the Holy Spirit to guide our speech. The effect of negative words concerning others has such a devastating effect that both Proverbs 18:8 and 26:22 tell us, *"The words of a talebearer are as wounds, and they go down into the innermost parts of the belly."* This means that they affect the very deep parts of an individual's emotions. Words can be as deadly as poison.

When the Holy Spirit is in control, the words we speak will be faith-filled and life-giving. The following scriptures further emphasize the importance of controlling what comes out of your mouth:

> *He that keepeth his mouth keepeth his life: but he that openeth wide his lips shall have destruction (Proverbs 13:3).*

> *Whoso keepeth his mouth and his tongue keepeth his soul from troubles (Proverbs 21:23).*

> *A wholesome tongue is a tree of life: but perverseness therein is a breach in the spirit (Proverbs 15:4).*

I am reminded of a man that I knew who always accepted whatever diagnosis the doctors gave him. He seemed to like the fact that he had an illness. Whenever I encountered him, he would talk about his latest diagnosed illness. He would speak as though his illnesses were a badge of honor. Needless to say, he was always sick. His death resulted from multiple illnesses. He was snared by constantly speaking of sickness. We do not have to accept a diagnosis as the ultimate word when God's Word tells us that Jesus took our sicknesses and carried our pains, and it is by His stripes that we are healed (Isaiah 53:5). We must speak according to His Word and set our course. I have had ailments and sicknesses at various times. I did not deny their existence, but I denied their right to stay in my body by confessing God's Word until healing came. I am a witness that speaking and believing God's Word works.

An outstanding 20th century example of an individual who spoke life instead of death, is John G. Lake. John Lake was a missionary to South Africa who had a ministry of healing. The book, *God's Generals*, tells of the time when John Lake was in South Africa and an epidemic of the bubonic plague broke out.[4] People were dying by the multitudes, and he was among those who helped to bury the dead. When the British relief ship arrived, which was sent with medical supplies and other necessities to aid those who were yet living, they were interested to know why Lake did not contract the disease. He explained to them he believed Romans 8:2 that says, *"For the law of the Spirit of life in Christ Jesus hath made me free from the law of sin and death."* Lake told them that when the germs came in contact with his body, they would die instantly because of "the law of the Spirit of life in Christ Jesus". He told them they could test him to see if this was not true. They took some live germs from a corpse and put it on his hand. When they viewed the results under the microscope sure enough, the germs died instantly on contact with his body. He spoke life to his body in the midst of so many who were dying from the plague. He neither feared the plague nor did he distance himself from those who had contracted it and were dying. He had confidence in the Word of God, which he believed implicitly and spoke unashamedly. He chose to speak life rather than death.

On a more personal note, I remember the time when I lived for a year in Colombia, South America as an exchange student. We were cautioned to be careful about the food and water we consumed because it could cause illness from bacteria of which we were not accustomed. I stood in faith on the scripture in 1Timothy 4:5 which speaks about food being *"sanctified by the word of God and prayer."* I would always speak the Word of God over my food as I blessed it each time I ate. I lived with a native family and had to eat what was set before me and could not pick and choose without being offensive to my hosts. Many of my friends, who were students from the U.S. and Europe, had numerous bouts with sicknesses caused by various strains of bacteria. I thank God for the power inherent in His Word because I never got sick or had any ailments from anything I ate or drank during my stay in Colombia.

You must speak life to obtain the promises made available to you in the Word of God. Hebrews the eleventh chapter tells of those who obtained the promises of God by faith. This can only be accomplished as you put the

Word of God in your heart, speak it out of your mouth, act accordingly, and allow it to accomplish the purposes of God for your life. *"Death and life are in the power of the tongue"*, and as Proverbs 18:21 affirms, you will receive the results of what you speak, whether for good or for bad.

Endnotes

1. Dr. Caroline Leaf, *Who Switched Off My Brain*, (South Africa: 2007), 115.
2. James Strong, *The New Strong's Exhaustive Concordance of the Bible*, Greek #692.
3. Ibid., Greek #4550.
4. Roberts Liardon, *God's Generals*, (Laguna Hills, California: Albury Publishing, 1996), 182-183.

5
TRUTH OR FACT?

To speak right words one must be aware that there is a difference between what we perceive as fact and what is true according to the Word. The dictionary defines "fact" as the actual existence of something, and "truth" as the thing that corresponds to fact or reality. However, the Bible defines truth as being what is correct or true according to the Word of God. We find this definition of truth in the words that Jesus prayed in John 17:17, when He said, *"Sanctify them through thy truth, thy word is truth."* Jesus established truth as being what the Word of God says. As believers, we walk by faith in the Word, and not what is evidenced through our circumstances, or our five senses. We must grasp this understanding to fully comprehend the importance of speaking truth as opposed to the facts of your situation.

Often, we speak according to what our situations and circumstances dictate. There are those who would say that if you are sick and confess that you are healed, you are not telling the truth. Others say, "Call a spade a spade", meaning, if you are sick, say that you are sick. Understand that speaking according to the truth of God's Word is not denying that you have a sickness but refusing its right to stay in your body. I am not saying that you are never to say that you are sick when you are, but after acknowledging such, if you choose to believe God's Word and pray the prayer of faith over yourself, then from that point on speak life to your body. If you speak according to what the Word says about healing, you are speaking truth. The following scriptures give us the truth of God's Word concerning our healing:

> *Surely he hath borne our griefs, and carried our sorrows: yet we did esteem him stricken, smitten of God, and afflicted. But he was wounded for our transgressions, he was bruised for our iniquities: the chastisement of our peace was upon him; and with his stripes we are healed (Isaiah 53:4-5).*

> *My son, attend to my words; incline thine ear unto my sayings. Let them not depart from thine eyes; keep them in the midst of thine heart. For they are life unto those that find them, and health to all their flesh (Proverbs 4:20-22).*

> *Who his own self bare our sins in his own body on the tree, that we, being dead to sins,*

> *should live unto righteousness: by whose stripes ye were healed (1Peter 2:24).*

Isaiah in chapter 53 verses 4 and 5 previously mentioned, prophesied the death of Jesus on the Cross and what it accomplished. In Proverbs 4, Solomon addresses the importance of words as life-giving and health sustaining. Peter reiterates Isaiah's prophecy, which was fulfilled in his day and now made available to all those who will believe in what Jesus accomplished. Are you going to accept the facts of your situation or the truth of God's Word? The scripture in Isaiah 53:1 asks, *"Who hath believed our report? and to whom is the arm of the Lord revealed?"* When the doctor says that you have a life-threatening illness and there is no hope for you, are you going to believe his facts or the truth of God's Word? It is God's truth on which you stand and of which you must speak. This makes the knowledge of the Word of God paramount in the stance that you take for your deliverance regardless of the situation.

In John chapter 8 verses 31 and 32 Jesus was talking to the Pharisees about truth and said to them, *"… If ye continue in my word, then are ye my disciples indeed; And ye shall know the truth, and the truth shall make you free."* From this statement we understand that knowing the truth depends on continuing in the Word. We continue in the Word by believing, speaking, and acting on what it says. We walk by faith when we believe the truth of the Word above everything else to the contrary. It is this truth that liberates us and causes us to inherit the promises of God.

Our Western way of thinking which is linked to the

Greek mindset often affects us where faith and speaking God's Word is concerned. This mindset is one which only believes what is factual evidence (meaning, what is apparent to the five senses) or what can be verified by scientific proof. The saying, "Seeing is believing" sums up this way of thinking. Biblical truth is the opposite as verified by Apostle Paul in 2 Corinthians 4:13, where he states, *"We having the same spirit of faith, according as it is written, I believed, and therefore have I spoken; we also believe, and therefore speak* (emphasis mine)." When we believe the truth of God's Word, we speak accordingly. The Psalmist David in Psalms 27:13 says, "*I had fainted,* **unless I had believed to see** *the goodness of the Lord in the land of the living* (emphasis mine)." This scripture emphasizes once again the Biblical truth of believing by faith for the desired result.

When I speak of taking God's truth as opposed to the facts of the situation, I am referring to choosing to believe God's Word as the standard of truth. There are those who are not sure that it is God's will to heal, deliver, or help them. They are basing their belief on their personal circumstances or what happened to sister or brother so and so. They use the phrase that God is sovereign. When they say this, they mean that maybe He will or maybe He will not save, heal, or deliver them. It is true that God is sovereign. However, He has stated in His Word what He will do according to His covenant with believers. Salvation from a life of sin, healing and deliverance are all a part of His covenant which is already settled, as revealed in the following scriptures:

> *My covenant will I not break, nor alter the thing that is gone out of my lips (Psalm 89:34).*
>
> *Know therefore that the Lord thy God, he is God, the faithful God, which keepeth covenant and mercy with them that love him and keep his commandments to a thousand generations (Deuteronomy 7:9).*
>
> *But now hath he obtained a more excellent ministry, by how much also he is the mediator of a better covenant, which was established upon better promises (Hebrews 8:6).*

Our responsibility as people of God is to believe His Word, and when we do so, He will fulfill it. There should be no "ifs, ands, and buts", about His willingness and ability to fulfill His Word. We do not serve a capricious God who will do something one minute and the next minute change his mind. Jesus said in Matthew 24:35, *"Heaven and earth shall pass away, but my words shall not pass away."* I find it both amusing and sobering that should His Word pass away, we would never know it because heaven and earth would cease to exist. We must be fully persuaded that God will fulfill His Word. This is the foundation on which we stand as we declare the truth of His Word in the face of the facts of our situation.

The patriarch Abraham is a noble example of one who trusted God to fulfill His Word. The scripture says about him, "*He staggered not at the promise of God through unbelief; but was strong in faith, giving glory to God; And being fully persuaded that, what He had promised, He was able also to perform* (Romans 4: 20-21)." God's Word as opposed to the facts of the situation is the story of Abraham. God told Abraham that he would make him the father of many nations and that his seed would be like the stars of heaven, the dust of the earth, and like the sand of the seashore for multitude. The fact of the situation was that Abraham was childless and old when God spoke these words to him. Not only was he old, but so was his wife Sarah who was well past the childbearing age. If they had looked only at the facts of the situation, they would never have believed the truth of God's Word that they would have a son. It was His truth which prevailed. Romans 4:17 in speaking of this time says, *(As it is written, I have made thee a father of many nations,) before him whom he believed, even God, who quickeneth the dead, and calleth those things which be not as though they were.* Notice the last part of this verse, "*...and calleth those things which be not as though they were.*" God spoke the truth into Abraham's life when he was old and his wife barren. He called those things that were not as though they were. Abraham believed God with the result that Sarah gave birth to Isaac. As followers of Christ, we emulate Him by speaking forth our healing and deliverance based on His Word. We can call things that are not as though they were. Once we believe the Word by accepting our healing, deliverance, etc., we must consistently speak what we believe.

Gideon would not have been successful in defeating the Midianites if he had placed his confidence in the facts of his present situation, instead of the truth of God's Word spoken to him by the angel. When the angel of the Lord appeared to Gideon, he was threshing wheat in the most unlikely of places, the winepress. He was not feeling encouraged that there was hope for Israel's situation. The angel spoke to him and made two significant declarations. In the first declaration, he told Gideon that God was with him. In the second one, he told him that he was a mighty man of valor. Gideon questioned the words of the angel based on his present situation. He wondered how God was with him in view of Israel's situation of having to hide food from the Midianites who had been confiscating everything of value. To add to his doubts of the angel's words was the fact that he did not come from a renowned tribe and certainly did not consider himself a mighty man of valor. However, as he became convinced of the truth of God's Word, he successfully defeated the Midianites and delivered Israel from their oppressors.

If we relate Gideon's story to the situation of people of God today, there is a striking parallel. If you are going through tests and trials to where there seems to be no hope, you must first of all know that God is with you because the scripture tells us in Hebrews 13:5, *"... for He hath said, I will never leave thee, nor forsake thee."* Second, you must understand that you are not **just** a conqueror, but **more than** a conqueror (Romans 8:37). God will deliver you according to Psalms 34:19 which says, *"Many are the afflictions of the righteous: but the Lord delivereth him out of them all."* The facts of your present situation do not change the truth of God's Word. It is this truth that you must speak into your situation. In the words of the angel to Gideon, you are a mighty person of valor regardless to how you feel or what your circumstances dictate. It is as you move forward speaking, believing, and acting on the truth of God's Word that your circumstances will change.

Another great example of accepting the truth of God over the facts of the situation is found in the example of the Shunammite woman in 2 Kings chapter 4. This woman and her husband were hospitable to the prophet Elisha by providing him a place to lodge when he would pass through their town. The prophet was pleased with the extent to which he was shown hospitality and wanted to do something special for this woman, so he asked if she would like for him to speak to the king or the captain of the army on her behalf. She graciously declined this offer. However, Gehazi, the servant of Elisha, told him that the woman and her husband were childless. Elisha called her in again and prophesied over her that at this season in the coming year, she would have a son. He prophesied according to what the Spirit of God showed him, and it happened exactly as he said.

As you continue reading this account you find that the woman's son died, and she set out to take him to the prophet. When her husband inquired about her going to the prophet, she responded with the words, *"It shall be well."* This lady spoke what she believed would come to pass. When the prophet saw her afar off, he told his servant to go and inquire about her welfare and that of her family. To his questions she responded, *"It is well"*. Once again, she spoke faith-filled words. When she reached the prophet, she told him that her child had died because she had an expectation that the man of God would resurrect her son. In Old Testament times the anointing was on the prophets to stand in their office and speak forth in prayer the will of God for the people. After praying and stretching himself over the child who was brought back to life, he presented him to his mother. This woman spoke the result that she desired and received it.

Your need may not be one of healing, but of finances. Whether it is a debt situation caused by unwise decisions or the fact that you just do not have enough money to make ends meet, God is present to help you. You must believe the truth of God's word over the facts of your situation and speak the same. There are various scriptures which speak to the truth of God's Word concerning finances among which are:

> *But my God shall supply all your need according to his riches in glory by Christ Jesus (Philippians 4:19).*

> *Give, and it shall be given unto you; good measure, pressed down, and shaken together, and running over, shall men give into your bosom. For with the same measure that ye mete withal it shall be measured to you again (Luke 6:38).*

> *The Lord is my Shepherd and I shall not want (Psalms 23:1).*

The Scriptures concur that we are to be good stewards of our finances and willingly give in tithes and offerings to support the work of God (Malachi 3:10-11). Sometimes after doing all of this, you find yourself in the situation of not having enough money. Instead of allowing the facts of the situation to dominate your speaking, you must replace this with the truth of God's Word and declare the promises of God over your finances.

God has many ways of supplying your needs. Your job is not your source, God is. I can testify that there have been times in my life where I could not seem to make ends meet. I was not in debt and was not making unwise financial decisions. I was also giving in tithes and offerings, which was why I spoke the Word of God over my situation, declaring His Word concerning finances. In various ways, God caused money to come into my hands. Sometimes it seemed as though I was down to the wire in needing to pay a bill or be able to buy something I needed. Without fail, God provided for me. I might add, I was not going around and telling everyone of my need. After committing my situation to the Lord I would speak His Word over my finances and believe Him for the increase according to Philippians 4:19 which says, *"But my God shall supply all your need according to his riches in glory by Christ Jesus."*

There are even times when I would take out my checkbook and prophesy abundance over it, "calling those things which be not as though they were." I can say that God has never failed to supply my needs. If you never have a trial of your faith, you will not develop spiritually. However, as you go through your trial by speaking God's truth concerning your situation, you will experience Him moving on your behalf and will be strengthened in your walk of faith.

The truth is that God desires us to prosper in all areas of our lives. The scripture tells us in 3 John 1:2, *"Beloved, I wish above all things that thou mayest prosper and be in health, even as thy soul prospereth."* This prosperity is only assured as we believe, speak, and act on the Word. You may be in a situation where people are attacking you verbally and maligning your name. The truth that you must bring into this situation is found in the following scriptures:

> *No weapon that is formed against thee shall prosper; and every tongue that shall rise against thee in judgment thou shalt condemn. This is the heritage of the servants of the Lord, and their righteousness is of me, saith the Lord (Isaiah 54:17).*

> *But I say unto you, Love your enemies, bless them that curse you, do good to them that hate you, and pray for them which despitefully use you, and persecute you (Matthew 5:44).*

> *When a man's ways please the Lord, he maketh even his enemies to be at peace with him (Proverbs 16:7).*

When we choose His truth over the facts of our situations, we will no longer be depressed and oppressed by the devil. Instead of saying what we have, we will have what we say according to the Word of God. We will no longer confuse the truth of God's Word with the facts of our circumstances. What we proclaim with our mouths will be established according to Job 22:28, which says, *"Thou shalt also decree a thing, and it shall be established unto thee: and the light shall shine upon thy way."* Decrees are words spoken which establish the reign of heaven in the earth based on God's Word. It also means, a formal and authoritative order having the force of law. When you put God's Word in your mouth through a decree, you are:

- coming into agreement with God's finished work at Calvary i.e. enforcing the victory won.
- announcing to the powers of darkness that God's Word is the first and final authority in all matters pertaining to you.
- creating an atmosphere for the manifestation of God's promises in your life.
- releasing the angels to work on your behalf.

You can decree words that God has spoken to you personally, and prophetic words spoken over you by others. The Apostle Paul told Timothy in 1Timothy 1:18, *"This charge I commit unto thee, son Timothy, according to the prophecies which went before on thee, that thou by them mightiest war a good warfare."* Timothy was to war with the prophecies spoken over him by speaking them into the atmosphere and not allowing anything to dissuade him.

When you decree prophetic words, it has the following effect:

- it keeps the prophetic word before you
- pushes past contrary situations and circumstances
- undergirds your faith in God's Word by keeping your faith in the word or promise active
- holds at bay the forces of darkness and anything to the contrary
- brings into manifestation the spoken word

As you will notice, decrees are just another form of confession. This is even more reason that idle words, jesting, and corrupt speech should be excluded from our conversation. We do not want negative results from wrong speaking.

During a time of great apostasy in Israel, God spoke through the prophet Isaiah concerning the state of the people. He described in minute detail the errant path the people had taken. They turned away from the covenant of God through unbelief and placed their confidence in themselves and the false gods of those around them. The scripture says that there was no justice and judgment, and *"truth had fallen in the street"* (Isaiah 59:14). This same situation is prevalent today in our society. The truth of the Word of God is being pushed back further and further by those in positions of authority, and people in general. The alarming aspect of this failure to believe the truth of God's Word is that it has spilled over into the church. Many people of God rely more on themselves and what man can do for them (meaning the doctor, lawyer, financial expert, etc.) than on what God can and will do as they place their confidence in the truth of His Word.

We must realize that God has not changed. He is the same yesterday, today and forever (Hebrews 13:8). He is looking for those who will put their trust in Him by believing His Word as stated in 2 Chronicles 16:9, *"For the eyes of the Lord run to and fro throughout the whole earth, to shew himself strong in the behalf of them whose heart is perfect toward him. .."* The word "perfect" is the Hebrew word *shalem* (shaw-lame) and means complete or whole.[1] When our heart is completely towards God, our confidence is securely placed in Him. This means when we are confronted with challenges in our lives, our priority is to find out what God's Word has to say concerning our situation and speak in agreement with the Word. I ask once again the question, "Do you believe the truth of God's Word or the facts of your situation?" If you believe God's truth you will speak and act accordingly.

Endnotes

1. James Strong, *The New Strong's Exhaustive Concordance of the Bible*, Hebrew #8003.

6
ANGELS LISTEN TO YOUR WORDS

As we approach the coming of the Lord Jesus, we will see a greater increase in the activity of angels in the earth realm. Angels are especially important to the establishment of God's kingdom in the earth. They have been active in the affairs of man throughout history as revealed in both the Old and New Testaments. The Greek word for angel is *aggelos (ang-el-os)* and means messenger or envoy.[1] Angels are present to help the Body of Christ fulfill the will of God in the earth. It is not unusual to hear of occasions where angels have appeared to believers in dreams or in person to deliver messages from God. You are probably wondering what part angels play in the matter of the words we speak. Continue this journey with me as we turn our focus to the relationship between the words we speak and the activity of angels.

First, let us look at what the Bible has to say about the function of angelic beings. The scripture says in Hebrews

1:13-14, *"But to which of the angels said he at any times, Sit on my right hand, until I make thine enemies thy footstool? Are they not all ministering spirits, sent forth to minister for them who shall be heirs of salvation?"* What this scripture tells us is that angels are ministering spirits who minister to us who are heirs of salvation. The word "ministering" is the Greek word *leitourgeikos (li-toorg-ik-os)* and means performance of service.[2] Angels perform a service to those who are in Christ. Psalms 91:11 tells us that God gives His angels charge over us to keep us in all our ways. This lets us know that they serve as our guardians and protectors.

In 2 Kings chapter 6, the servant of Elisha became afraid because of the great army that surrounded them, sent by the king of Syria to capture the prophet Elisha. The prophet was not in the least bit worried because he could see into the supernatural realm the host of angels sent to protect him. He asked God to open the eyes of his servant so he too could see this angelic host of protection that surrounded them. The scripture says in 2 Kings 6:17, *"And Elisha prayed, and said, Lord, I pray thee, open his eyes, that he may see. And the Lord opened the eyes of the young man; and he saw: and, behold, the mountain was full of horses and chariots of fire round about Elisha."* What God allowed the servant to see was the host of warring angels commissioned for their protection. Psalms 34:7 verifies this function of angels when it says, *"The angel of the Lord encampeth round about them that fear Him, and delivereth them."* Angels not only protect, but they also deliver us in difficult situations as this portion of scripture so aptly states.

We can cooperate with the ministry of angels as we do

the work of the Kingdom. Our part is to speak the Word, and the angels will minister according to the words we speak, as revealed in Psalms 103:20-21: *"Bless the Lord, ye his angels, that excel in strength, that do his commandments, hearkening unto the voice of his word. Bless ye the Lord, all ye his hosts; ye ministers of his, that do his pleasure."* If you will notice in verse 20, it says that the angels hearken or pay attention to the voice of God's word. We speak the Word, and the angels are dispatched to do what is necessary to bring the Word to pass in our lives. From the scripture in verse 21, we also understand that that the angels bless the Lord in worship and service as well as do His pleasure.

The prophet Daniel is another example of one who received the ministry of angels. Daniel was among the children of Judah who were taken captive by the Babylonian king, Nebuchadnezzar. In chapter one of his book, you find that because of the blessing of the Lord on him and his three companions, Hananiah, Mishael, and Azariah, they were placed among the king's learned men. In the process of time, Daniel was promoted to a chief place in government as he interpreted dreams and served with an excellent spirit in the King's court. Because of his dedication to God, he was given revelations. One such revelation occurred in chapter 9. When Daniel knew that the 70 years of Israel's captivity was ending (through his reading the prophecy of Jeremiah), he sought the Lord with prayers and fasting (Daniel 9:3). While he was praying and confessing the sins of the nation, the angel Gabriel appeared to him and gave him revelation concerning the end of the captivity and significant future events (Daniel 9:20-27). Daniel's words in prayer activated the release of the angel Gabriel to bring revelation important to Israel's future.

Chapter 10 of Daniel brings us to another angelic appearance. This encounter occurred in the third year of the reign of the Persian King Cyrus. Daniel had received a revelation from God and was in a time of fasting when the heavenly messenger appeared. The scripture says in Daniel 10:4-5, *And in the four and twentieth day of the first month, as I was by the side of the great river, which is Hiddekel; Then I lifted up mine eyes, and looked, and behold a certain man clothed in linen, whose loins were girded with fine gold of Uphaz:* Biblical scholars view this occurence as a theophany of the pre-incarnate Christ more so than an angel. Notice what he said to Daniel in verse 12, "*Then said he unto me, Fear not, Daniel: for from the first day that thou didst set thine heart to understand, and to chasten thyself before thy God, thy words were heard, and **I am come for thy words*** (emphasis mine)." There is no doubt that the words that Daniel spoke in prayer precipitated the heavenly encounter. Daniel's words agreed with the Word of God for the nation of Israel. Otherwise, a heavenly messenger (be it the pre-incarnate Christ or an angel), would not have been dispatched to give him revelation. In like manner, the words we speak in accordance with God's Word activate angels.

Do the words you speak agree with God's Word for your situation? If so, they activate the angels. When you release words into the atmosphere that agree with God's Word, the angels are released to bring that word to pass because they pay attention to God's Word (Psalm 103:20). Likewise, words that you speak contrary to the Word of

God which are frivolous and full of unbelief hinder them. In fact, negative speaking activates the demonic realm which operates to bring to pass misfortune and adverse circumstances.

Angels can bring messages from God to people. The angel Gabriel was sent to Mary, the mother of Jesus, with the news that she would bring forth a son. She inquired how this could be since she was a virgin. After hearing that the Holy Spirit would overshadow her, she did not draw back in unbelief but spoke the words, *"Be it unto me according to thy word* (Luke 1:38)." That she spoke in this manner opened the way for the prophecy to be fulfilled on her behalf. The angelic host could work to bring to pass God's will for her and for all mankind since she would bring forth Jesus, the Savior of the world. Mary afterwards spoke what she would receive because of her belief in the words of the angel when she said, *"For he hath regarded the low estate of his handmaiden: for, behold, from henceforth all generations shall call me blessed* (Luke 1:48)." This declaration of Mary has been true down through the generations, as she has been highly esteemed and venerated for giving birth to Jesus Christ.

Angels were prominent in the Biblical record of Jesus' birth and at various times during His earthly ministry. The book of Matthew records three different times that angels appeared to Joseph. The first time was when Joseph was told to take Mary as his wife (Matthew 1:20). The second occasion occurred when he was warned to flee to Egypt from Herod, who was killing the male babies in an attempt to do away with the promised King of the Jews (Matthew 2:13). Finally, it was an angel who let Joseph know when it was safe to return to Nazareth after the death of Herod (Matthew 2:19-20). Angels also appeared to the wisemen and shepherds. In one account after another, angels were actively involved in the birth and life of Jesus.

As we follow this pattern of angelic intervention in the affairs of men, we find that Peter was arrested by Herod Agrippa and imprisoned to be executed (Acts 12:1-4). The scripture intimates that prayer was made continually by the church for him. These prayers resulted in an angel appearing to Peter in the prison and leading him to freedom. The words that the people of God spoke in prayer brought about the intervention of the angel. Believers in the New Testament church must have been acquainted with angelic visitations because they initially supposed that it was Peter's angel standing at the door instead of Peter after his release from prison.

In Acts chapter 16, Paul and Silas were imprisoned for preaching the Gospel. Scripture records that they sang praises to God (Acts 16:25). These praises extolling God's greatness, faithfulness and delivering power were released into the atmosphere. The scripture tells us, *"And suddenly there was a great earthquake, so that the foundations of the prison were shaken: and immediately all the doors were opened, and everyone's bands were loosed* (Acts 16:26)." Paul and Silas could have lamented their situation and complained with negative words which would have delayed angelic intervention; instead, they chose to sing praises to God and were miraculously delivered.

When the apostle John describes the revelation unveiled to him on the isle of Patmos, he records what was spoken by the angel who said, *"And they overcame him by the blood of the Lamb, and by the word of their testimony; and they loved not their lives unto the death (Revelation 12:11)."* Notice that *"the word of their testimony"* was included as one of the factors in overcoming the devil. These testimonies contained deliverances accomplished as the Word of God was spoken, believed, and adhered to by many who gave their lives for the cause of Christ. As 21st Century believers, we too can testify of God's goodness in our lives as we overcome Satan by the power of God's Word.

In chapter 5 of this book, I referred to the scripture in Job 22:28, which says, *"Thou shalt also decree a thing, and it shall be established unto thee: and the light shall shine upon thy ways."* I stated that angels listen to the decrees you make. If what you decree lines up with the Word of God, angels are activated to carry out your decree. Contrariwise, if what you decree does not adhere to the Word of God, they have nothing to work with.

On this subject of angels listening to your words, I would like to emphasize that when you pray in tongues, or as it is sometimes called, praying in the Spirit, the words you speak are powerful and impacting. In 1 Corinthians 14:2, the scripture says, *"For he that speaketh in an unknown tongue speaketh not unto men, but unto God: for no man understandeth him; howbeit in the spirit he speaketh mysteries."* When you pray in this manner, you are speaking forth the will of God on your behalf and for whatever else the Spirit of God directs. The words you speak into the atmosphere bypass your natural mind and are spoken from your spirit. This is spirit to spirit communication. There is no misdirecting of these words. As they ascend to God, angels are dispatched to do God's bidding on your behalf or that of the individual or situation about which you are praying.

I recall a time in my Christian walk when I was going through some tough challenges. Not even knowing what it was called, I prayed in tongues. Over a short period of time, my situation changed for the better. I believe that I activated the angels of the Lord through such speaking, and they worked to bring about victory in my situation. From that point forward I have continued the practice of praying in tongues. Praying in tongues will release the will of God in your life. Discipline yourself to regularly pray in this manner.

The accounts I have listed here are just some of the examples of the role angels play as we speak God's Word over the circumstances in our lives, and as we intercede for others. It should be quite clear by now that the words we speak affect both the natural and supernatural realms. Whether or not we see angels, we know according to God's Word that they exist and are at work on our behalf. We activate them as we release our words into the atmosphere. We can tie their hands by always speaking in the negative. Are you going through a period in your life where it appears your prayers are ineffective? Do a quick check on the words you allow to come out of your mouth. Are you speaking words of life? You have angels assigned to you, but they can only respond in accordance with God's Word.

After reading what I have written within these pages, you can no longer claim ignorance as a reason for speaking contrary to God's Word. He holds you accountable for what you know. Why not allow Him to bring to manifestation those things you desire by speaking the Word? The angels are present and active as you do so. Once again, you are the one who will decide the extent to which you experience God's promises fulfilled in your life. With this understanding, make sure that your words agree with God's Word so that the angels can be activated to bring them to pass.

Endnotes

1. James Strong, *The New Strong's Exhaustive Concordance of the Bible*, Greek #32.
2. Ibid., Greek #3010.

7
SPEAK THE WORD DAILY

Daily confession of the Word of God should be the normal way of life for the people of God. As a believer, you should not allow a day to pass without speaking the Word over yourself and over the situations that arise in your life. If this has not been your practice, then you should begin today to make it so. Speaking the Word helps faith to come because faith comes by hearing the Word of God. When you are speaking the Word of God and hearing yourself speak, you are causing faith to come. It is, as faith comes that you obtain the promises of God and get the victory over adverse circumstances according to 1 John 5:4 which says, *"For whatsoever is born of God overcometh the world: and this is the victory that overcometh the world, even our faith."*

We live in a world of constant distractions, which makes it quite easy to get caught up in the busyness of life. As believers, we must take the time to study God's Word and speak it often. As God told Joshua, "*This book of the law shall not depart out of thy mouth; but thou shalt meditate therein day and night, that thou mayst observe to do according to all that is written therein: for then thou shalt make thy way prosperous, and then thou shalt have good success* (Joshua 1:8)." Whether you are believing God in a certain area or not, you can speak the Word of God concerning who you are in Christ, and what you have in Him as a believer. Do not wait until you are in a test or trial to confess the Word, make this a daily practice. It will build strength into your spirit and give you an arsenal of spiritual weaponry to use against the attacks of the devil.

God delights in our speaking His Word to one another according to Malachi 3 16, "*Then they that feared the Lord spake often one to another: and the Lord hearkened, and heard it, and a book of remembrance was written before him for them that feared the Lord, and that thought upon his name.*" Speaking the Word is how we encourage ourselves and others in the Christian walk. I began the practice of daily confessing the Word years ago. I was on a quest to discover how to live the overcoming life in Christ. This brought me to a study of faith in God and what it meant to believe the Word of God and apply it in my life. I would write down scriptures and read them daily until I had memorized them. If I were going through a test or trial, I would find those scriptures appropriate to my situation, and speak them at various times throughout the day. In driving to and from work, I would use this time to pray and speak God's Word.

Speaking the Word daily has revolutionized my prayer life. No longer do I just mouth words in making known my requests to the Lord, but I pray the specific word of God for my particular need. If I am in a situation that causes me to be fearful, I pray the scriptures as follows; "Lord you did not give me a spirit of fear, but of power of love and of a sound mind. Therefore, I rest in You, knowing that at what time I am afraid, I will trust in You (2 Timothy 1:7; Psalms 56:3)." I pray the promises of God for myself and others during my times of intercession. Praying the Word brings results. God honors His Word. Jeremiah 1:12 says, *"Then said the Lord to me, You have seen well, for I am alert and active, watching over My word to perform it* (AMP)." Whether I am praying in private or public, I pray the Word.

The Lord once gave me an inward vision in which I saw a wrecking ball (attached to a crane) demolish a structure. The more this ball hit the structure, the more unstable it became until it finally came crashing down. God said to me that our prayers when prayed according to the Word are like a wrecking ball. Continuous speaking the Word loosens the foundation of strongholds and contrary situations in our lives until they are finally demolished. This vision underscores the fact that we must be persistent in speaking the Word until we receive the desired manifestation. The scripture in Isaiah 55:11, which has been quoted previously, confirms the surety of the manifestation when it says, *"So shall my word be that goeth forth out of my mouth: it shall not return unto me void, but it shall accomplish that which I please, and it shall prosper in the thing whereto I sent it."*

If you are among those who do not speak according to the Word, you can begin today to turn this around. Start where you are and make a conscious decision to speak according to the Word. Begin to change "idle words" to words that minister life. Refrain from saying the opposite of what you mean. Instead of being "tickled to death", be "tickled to happiness." Instead of "loving someone to death", "love them to life." You must understand that since negative ways of speaking have been developed over time, it will take an intentional effort on your part to reverse this pattern. You must believe for yourself the scripture in Philippians 4:13, which says, *"I can do all things through Christ which strengtheneth me."* This may mean that you will talk less than you have in the past and concentrate more on speaking in agreement with God's Word.

Sometimes, instead of speaking idle words, it is better to say nothing. When Joshua crossed the Jordan to conquer Jericho, he followed what God instructed him to do in not allowing the people to say anything as they marched around the walls once a day for seven days and then seven times on the final day when they shouted and the walls came down. This is recorded in Joshua 6:10: *"And Joshua had commanded the people, saying, Ye shall not shout, nor make any noise with your voice, neither shall any word proceed out of your mouth, until the day I bid you shout; then shall ye shout."* There is no telling what words the Israelites would have spoken had they been allowed to carry on conversations as they marched. God did not want them to release words into the atmosphere that would negate the victory that He planned for them. The sentries on the walls of Jericho could not figure out what was happening because the Israelites were not saying anything. In the same vein, when you refrain from releasing negative words into the atmosphere, the devil and his demons have nothing to grasp and use against you. If anything, they will run in terror as you resist them with the spoken Word of God.

One point I want to emphasize is that, it is not what you say once or twice that becomes a reality, but what you continually say whether for good or bad that will come to pass. I personally know of adults who were injured by negative words that were constantly spoken to them when they were children. These words got down into their heart and produced wrong thinking patterns and complexes about their ability to perform certain tasks or about their physical appearance in relation to others. They internalized these words and agreed with them to the extent that they spoke these things about themselves. The scripture in Proverbs 23:7 says, *".... For as he thinketh in his heart, so is he."* They hindered themselves from success in many areas of their lives by believing and acting on the negative words spoken against them.

As you strive to change your way of speaking to that of confessing the Word, do not make yourself a nuisance by correcting what everyone else is saying, just make sure you are speaking in a right manner. It is in this area of correcting others that criticism has been leveled against those who make a practice of speaking the Word. It is unnecessary to make everyone around you speak right unless you are a part of a group of believers who have focused on speaking life-giving words by helping one another. In such a case, it is acceptable to offer correction one to another. Otherwise, you need to concentrate on personally speaking in a wholesome manner. In my nuclear family, we decided years ago to eliminate from our speech the common sayings of our culture that are racial slurs against other nationalities. When any of us makes such comments, we are reminded by the rest that we do not speak in this manner. Right speaking must affect your entire conversation. If you love others as the Word of God commands, you will not speak disparaging words against them.

When someone speaks negative words to me or says the wrong thing about my situation, I merely speak the opposite without responding offensively. For example, if someone tells me I am lucky, I say, "You know, I am blessed". If they try to define who I am in a negative manner, I say who I am according to the Word. I do not allow people to define who I am. I allow the Word to define who I am, because I am who the Word of God says that I am, which is:

- The righteousness of God in Christ Jesus (2 Corinthians 5:21).
- More than a conqueror through Him that loves me (Romans 8:37).
- I am the salt of the earth and light in a dark world (Matthew 5:13-14).
- I am the head and not the tail, above only and not beneath (Deuteronomy 28:13).

There are many other scriptures that I can add to this list. The point is, eventually people get the message and understand that I will not agree with negative statements spoken about me but will replace them with the positivism of God's Word.

Being an individual of wholesome speech does not mean that you put yourself in a straitjacket by being unable to express how you feel about your situation or circumstances. It is unnecessary for you to broadcast your feelings or the details of a test or trial to everyone with whom you come in contact. There are among the people of God those with whom you can express your feelings, and who will stand in faith with you as you believe God. You must use caution in telling others what you are going through, because there are individuals who will, by their unbelief, hinder your faith in God. Once you have expressed your feelings to those who will agree with you in prayer, fill your mouth with the Word of God and allow your faith in the Word to change the situation.

Speaking in line with the Word does not mean that you cannot have fun and enjoy times of laughter as you fellowship with others. Proverbs 17:22 says, "*A merry heart doeth good like a medicine: but a broken spirit drieth the bones.*" There are those who feel that a long face and always being of a sober countenance is a sign of holiness. However, if you are a person of holiness, the joy of the Lord will well up in you so that you cannot help but smile and have a great time sharing this joy with others. In fact, one of the ways to get through trials is to laugh in the face of contrary circumstances because God "*always causes us to triumph in Christ*" *(2 Corinthians 2:14)*. Instead of "carrying burdens", place them on the Lord as you continue on your way with a song in your heart and praise on your lips. If you act in this manner, people will ask to know your secret of joy amid life's storms.

In over forty years of ministry, I have witnessed abuses to the message of faith and those who believe in speaking right according to God's Word. Often these abuses have occurred because people have not understood the dynamics of faith and confession. Some have tried to imitate others' faith and shipwrecked. Others have only given mental assent to the Word, without allowing it to get into their heart and bring forth the desired result. There are also those who have neglected to speak the truth in the face of the facts of their circumstances for fear of what they perceive as telling a lie. I reiterate, truth is what God's Word says, whereas facts are the reality of your present situation or circumstance. It is God's Word which is the superior reality and must become so in your life.

It is imperative that you daily feed your spirit with the Word of God. Psalms 1 calls the man blessed who meditates in the Word day and night. This Psalm goes on to say in verse 3, *"And he shall be like a tree planted by the rivers of water that brings forth his fruit in his season; his leaf also shall not wither; and whatsoever he doeth shall prosper."* Daily meditation in the Word will cause you to prosper because what you say, and what you do, reflects the Word you have placed in your heart. I have included a list of scriptures in the Appendix that will help you in daily confession of the Word.

Speaking the Word is like planting seeds in a garden. You plant the seed and continue to water it. As time progresses, the seed yields the desired fruit. The scripture states in Mark 4: 28, *"For the earth bringeth forth fruit of herself; first the blade, then the ear, after that the full corn in the ear."* Just like a seed that you plant, you build your faith as you continue to speak the Word. You will receive the desired manifestation because of speaking, believing, and acting in agreement with God's Word.

The result of abuses to faith and speaking the Word has made many believers shy away from confessing the word and being open to any teaching on the subject. We must not "throw the baby out with the bath water." We please God when we walk by faith. Hebrews 11:6 says, *"Without faith it is impossible to please God."* Granted, some have made mistakes, but this does not mean that confessing the Word is invalid or that "there is nothing to it." You have read throughout this book the many scriptural references validating the importance of speaking the Word. Confession of the Word is working in my life and the lives of those who have chosen to make a practice of speaking the Word and allowing the results to be manifested in their lives.

We must seek God for a better understanding of His Word and continue to go from faith to faith in Him according to Romans 1:17: *For therein is the righteousness of God revealed from faith to faith: as it is written, The just shall live by faith.* As believers, faith should be our lifestyle. The scripture just quoted in Romans is found in Habakkuk 2:4, and also reiterated in Galatians 3:11 and Hebrews 10:38. It is not by accident that the phrase, *"the just shall live by faith"* is on the pages of God's Word four different times and appears in both the Old and New Testaments. This repetition emphasizes the importance that God places on a lifestyle of faith. As stated earlier, we please God as we walk by faith and He has obligated Himself to respond, as stated in Numbers 23:19, *"God is not a man, that he should lie; neither the son of man, that he should repent: hath he said, and shall he not do it? or hath he spoken, and shall he not make it good?"* As a God of covenant who cannot lie, He will fulfill His Word.

Keeping the Word of God in our heart and on our lips is vitally important if we are to live in God's best. The words we speak can bring life or death, blessing, or cursing, which reminds me of Moses' final warning to the children of Israel before entering the Promised Land. He said to them in Deuteronomy 30:19, *"I call heaven and earth to record this day against you, that I have set before you life and death, blessing and cursing: therefore choose life, that both thou and thy seed may live."* God has given us His Word not just to bless ourselves but also to bless others. If more of the people of God would make a practice of daily speaking the Word, we would see not only changes in our lives but also in our communities and nation. We would witness the continuation of the book of Acts with signs, wonders, and miracles following the preaching and teaching of the Word. There must arise boldness in the people of God so radical that the world will know by our speech and actions that nothing can stop us from bringing forth the will of God on earth as it is in Heaven.

God is at work in our midst. He desires to show Himself mighty on behalf of those who will believe Him and declare His Word to the ends of the earth. Will you be a part of this great company? Carefully ponder this question because an answer of yes means that God's Word will be in your mouth as you speak it over your life situations and over the lives of others to bring salvation, healing, deliverance and wholeness to a world in desperate need of the presence of God. So, dear reader, I leave you with this admonition, "Watch what you say because what you continually say and believe will determine your destiny."

APPENDIX A
SCRIPTURES FOR DAILY CONFESSION OF THE WORD

The following scriptures have been placed in this appendix to aid you in daily confession of the Word of God. They are not all-inclusive but will get you started in speaking God's Word. They have been personalized so that as you speak them out; you agree with and declare what Jesus said, releasing the power of the Word into the surrounding atmosphere. Feel free to add scriptures and make your own set of confessions. Meditation and memorization of these scriptures will also help to strengthen your faith in God. May you be blessed as you make a practice of daily speaking the Word of God.

WHO I AM IN CHRIST: I am who the Word of God says that I am:

- I am a new creation in Christ Jesus, old things have passed away and all things have become new (2 Corinthians 5:17).

- I am an heir of God and a joint heir with Jesus Christ (Romans 8:17).
- I am seated together in heavenly places in Christ Jesus (Ephesians 2:6).
- I am more than a conqueror through Him that loves me (Romans 8:37).
- I am the temple of the Holy Ghost; I am not my own, I am bought with a price (1Corinthians 6:19).
- I am a believer and these signs do follow me; I cast out devils; I speak with new tongues; I take up serpents; If I drink any deadly thing it will not hurt me; I lay hands on the sick and they do recover (Mark 16:17-18).
- I am the salt of the earth and light in this dark world (Matthew 5:13,14)

WHAT I HAVE IN CHRIST:

- I have authority over all the power of the enemy (Luke 10:19).
- I overcome by the Blood of the Lamb and the word of my testimony; I love not my life to the death (Revelation 12:11).
- I have a better covenant based on better promises (Hebrews 8:6).
- I have the peace of God that passes all understanding that keeps my heart and mind through Christ Jesus (Philippians 4:7).
- I have a sound mind. I have the mind of Christ (2Timothy 1:7; 1Corinthians 2:16).

- I have been delivered from the power of darkness and translated into the Kingdom of the Son of His love (Colossians 1:13).
- In Him I live and move and have my being (Acts 17:28).

CONFESSIONS FOR HEALING

- He sent His Word and healed me (Psalm 107:20).
- Christ has redeemed me from the curse of the law (Colossians 3:13).
- Who his own self bare our sins in His own body on the tree, that we being dead to sins, should live unto righteousness by whose stripes ye were healed (1Peter 2:24).
- God forgives all my iniquities and heals all my diseases (Psalms 103:3).
- I shall not die, but live and declare the works of the Lord (Psalms 118:17).
- But He was wounded for my transgressions, He was bruised for my iniquities, the chastisement of my peace was upon Him; and with His stripes I am healed (Isaiah 53:5).
- God's Word is life unto me for I have found it, and health to all my flesh (Proverbs 4:22).

CONFESSIONS FOR FINANCIAL PROSPERITY

- But my God shall supply all my need according

to His riches in glory by Christ Jesus (Philippians 4:19).
- I give and it is given to me good measure, pressed down, shaken together and running over shall men give into my bosom (Luke 6:38)
- The Lord has pleasure in the prosperity of His servant and Abraham's blessings are mine (Psalms 35:27; Galatians 3:14).
- I hearken diligently unto the voice of the Lord God and observe and do His commandments so that His blessings come on me and overtake me. My basket and store are blessed; I am the head and not the tail, above only and not beneath. I lend and do not borrow (Deuteronomy 28:1-2, 5, 13).
- The Lord is my Shepherd and I shall not want (Psalms 23:1).
- I give in tithes and offerings and God opens the windows of heaven and pours me out blessings that I do not have room enough to receive; God rebukes the devourer for my sake (Malachi 3:10, 11).
- God gives me the power to get wealth, that He might establish His covenant (Deuteronomy 8:18).

CONFESSIONS FOR OBTAINING GOD'S WISDOM

- Jesus is made unto me wisdom, righteousness, sanctification, and redemption; therefore, I have the wisdom of God and I am the

righteousness of God in Christ Jesus (1 Corinthians 1:30; 2 Corinthians 5:21).
- I am filled with the knowledge of the Lord's will in all wisdom and spiritual understanding (Colossians 1:9).
- The Spirit of truth abides in me and teaches me all things, and He guides me into all truth (John 16:13).
- I trust in the Lord with all my heart and I lean not to my own understanding. In all of my ways I acknowledge Him and He directs my path (Proverbs 3:5-6).
- I follow the Good Shepherd, and know His voice. The voice of a stranger I will not follow (St. John 10:4-5).
- Wisdom is the principal thing therefore I get wisdom, and in my getting, I get understanding (Proverbs 4:7).
- God gives to me wisdom as I ask Him in faith, nothing wavering (James 1:5-6).

CONFESSIONS FOR OVERCOMING FEAR

- God has not given me the spirit of fear, but of power, love and a sound mind (2 Timothy 1:7)
- I am far from oppression and fear does not come nigh me (Isaiah 54:14).
- As He is, so am I in this world. There is no fear in love; but perfect love casteth out fear (1John 4:17-18).
- No weapon that is formed against me shall

prosper, and every tongue that rises against me in judgment I shall condemn. This is my heritage as a servant of the Lord and my righteousness is of Him (Isaiah 54:17).
- The Lord is my light and my salvation; whom shall I fear? The Lord is the strength of my life; of whom shall I be afraid? (Psalms 27:1)
- I will not fear for the Lord has redeemed me. When I pass through the waters, He will be with me, and through the rivers, they shall not overflow me: when I walk through the fire I shall not be burned; neither shall the flame kindle upon me (Isaiah 43:1-2).
- I will not be afraid or dismayed, for the Lord my God is with me (Joshua 1:9).

CONFESSIONS FOR SPEAKING WHOLESOME WORDS

- I will let no corrupt speech come out of my mouth but that which is good to the use of edifying that it may minister grace to the hearers (Ephesians 4:29).
- In my tongue is the law of kindness (Proverbs 31:26).
- I will let my speech be always with grace seasoned with salt that I may know how I ought to answer every man (Colossians 4:6).
- I will speak God's Word because His Words are spirit and they are life (John 6:63).

- Death and life are in the power of my tongue therefore I choose to speak life (Proverbs 18:21).
- I will let the words of my mouth and the meditations of my heart be acceptable unto God who is my Strength and my Redeemer (Psalms 19:14).
- I keep my tongue from evil and my lips that they speak no guile (1Peter 3:10).

BIBLIOGRAPHY

Leaf, Dr. Caroline, *Who Switched Off My Brain: Controlling Toxic Thoughts and Emotions*. Rivonia, South Africa, Switch on Your Brain Organisation LTD, 2007.

Liardon, Robert. *God's Generals*. Laguna Hills, California: Albury Publishing, 1996.

Otis, George, with Norman Williams. *Terror at Tenerife*. Van Nuys, California: Bible Voice, 1977.

Scofield, C.I. Rev. *The Scofield Reference Bible*. New York, New York: Oxford University Press, 1909.

Strong, James, *The New Strong's Exhaustive Concordance of the Bible*. Nashville: Thomas Nelson Publishers, 1990.

Vine, W.E. *Vine's Expository Dictionary of Old and New Testament Words*. Old Tappan, N.J.: Fleming H. Revell, 1981.

ABOUT THE AUTHOR

Pamela J. Thomas is an author, ordained minister, and a consummate pursuer of the deeper insights of God. She is president of Christ for the World Ministries and CEO of Ruach Press, LLC. She is dedicated to teaching training and equipping individuals for Kingdom service. Her focus is on the prophetic, deliverance, healing, and prayer aspects of the apostolic calling of the church. Her passion is to release individuals into their God-ordained destiny by means of the spoken and written word.

Pamela has traveled in ministry to countries in Africa, Asia, the Middle East, Europe, and South America. She holds a B.A. degree from Purdue University in Sociology and Spanish, and an M.A. degree from Indiana University in Sociology. She has studied in Colombia, South America, as a Fulbright scholar.

She desires to publish material that will be a blessing to the body of Christ. In addition to the stories she will write, there are others who have stories which, through Ruach Press, she will help them bring to life. Besides *Watch What You Say: The Power of the Spoken Word, Revised*, she has written *A Practical Guide to Altar Ministry*, and *How to Protect Your Mind*. She has two books that are forthcoming, *Meditations in the Word: Book 1 and Book 2*.

CONTACT INFORMATION

Pamela J. Thomas
P.O. Box 55502
Indianapolis, Indiana 46220
Email: pamt320@sbcglobal.net

www.ingramcontent.com/pod-product-compliance
Lightning Source LLC
Chambersburg PA
CBHW070942080526
44589CB00013B/1612